Wishful Thinking

WISHFUL THINKING

Cartoons by David Sipress

PERENNIAL LIBRARY

HARPER & ROW, PUBLISHERS, New York

Cambridge, Philadelphia, San Francisco, Washington
London, Mexico City, São Paulo, Singapore, Sydney

Portions of this work have appeared in *Boston Phoenix*, *Psychology Today*, *Chicago*, *New Woman*, *Lear's*, and *Writer's Digest*.

Designer: Woods End Studio

Library of Congress Cataloging-in-Publication Data

Sipress, David.
  Wishful thinking.

  1. American wit and humor, Pictorial.   I. Title.
NC1429.S532A4   1987   741.5'973   86-45150
ISBN 0-06-096082-5 (pbk.)

87   88   89   90   91   **HC**   10   9   8   7   6   5   3   2

For my friends
and my family

Wishful Thinking

Mother, teach me to shop.

SIPRESS

SIPRESS

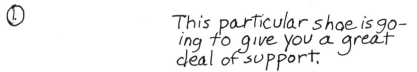

SIPRESS

I do like myself, Cheryl. It's my body I hate.

SIPRESS

She just had a body perm.

SIPRESS

SIPRESS

SIPRESS

I just know that at this very moment, some guy at the I.R.S. is picking up my tax return and he's putting it in the audit pile.

SIPRESS

1.

2.

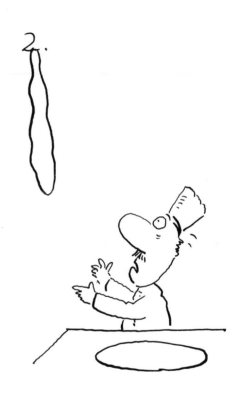

SIPRESS

SIPRESS

SIPRESS

SIPRESS

Try to think of it as a free meal.

I forget. Are we going to work or are we coming home?

A Christmas Cartoon:

① Merry Christmas! Boy, what a joke! Here I am all alone on Christmas Eve, a lonely guy with no family to be with any more! Everybody else is laughing and having a great time and I'm lying here by myself with my stupid little present that I got for myself there under my dumb little tree! Gee, I wonder if I can guess what it is?? Well, I'll be opening it tommorrow, _all alone_, while everbody else in the world is with their families. Boy! How miserable can life get?!!

②

Wake up, Jerry! This is the Ghost of Christmas Past...

Jerry's Father
Young Jerry
Uncle Fred
Jerry's Mother
Other Relatives arguing!

Zen Cartoon:

SIPRESS

'Hi. I'm calling you at random to give you 3 million dollars, but since you're not at home, I'm going to call somebody else.'
SIPRESS

If this piece of paper lands in that trash barrel, I'm going to walk into Emilio's and meet the man I'm going to marry.
Emilio's
SIPRESS

SIPRESS

SIPRESS

"STELLA!!!"

SIPRESS

SIPRESS

SIPRESS

SIPRESS

Take a break, Marvin! Take a break!!

Have I forgotten anything?
HOW TO BE HAPPY
HOW TO GET RICH
HOW TO DANCE
HOW TO LOOK GREAT
HOW TO SWIM
HOW TO MEET MEN
HOW TO BE YOU
How To Relax
HOW TO BE THIN
HOW TO GET A JOB
HAVE GOOD Sex
SIPRESS

SIPRESS

SIPRESS

So I hit the ball, so it goes in the hole, so I get all excited for a minute... So big deal.

SIPRESS

What if you're just a dog and not someone's pet per se?